JOHNNY APPLESEED

A TALL TALE RETOLD AND ILLUSTRATED BY
STEVEN KELLOGG

MORROW JUNIOR BOOKS/NEW YORK

Printed in the United States of America.   7 8 9 10 11 12 13 14 15 16

Library of Congress Cataloging-in-Publication Data

Kellogg, Steven.
   Johnny Appleseed/Steven Kellogg.
      p.   cm.
   Summary: Presents the life of John Chapman, better known as Johnny Appleseed, describing his love of nature, his kindness to animals, and his physical fortitude.
   ISBN 0-688-06417-5.   ISBN 0-688-06418-3 (lib. bdg.)
   1. Appleseed, Johnny, 1774-1845—Juvenile literature.   2. Apple growers—United States—Biography—Juvenile literature.   3. Frontier and pioneer life—Middle West—Juvenile literature.   [1. Appleseed, Johnny, 1774-1845.   2. Apple growers.   3. Frontier and pioneer life.]   I. Title.
SB63.C46K45   1988   634'.11'0924—dc19   [B]   [92]   87-27317   CIP

Love
to my friends
Lenny, Margaret,
and their wonderful family,
Lenny and Leah

John Chapman, who later became known as Johnny Appleseed, was born on September 26, 1774, when the apples on the trees surrounding his home in Leominster, Massachusetts, were as red as the autumn leaves.

John's first years were hard. His father left the family to fight in the Revolutionary War, and his mother and his baby brother both died before his second birthday.

By the time John turned six, his father had remarried and settled in Longmeadow, Massachusetts. Within a decade their little house was overflowing with ten more children.

Nearby was an apple orchard. Like most early
American families, the Chapmans picked their apples in
the fall, stored them in the cellar for winter eating, and
used them to make sauces, cider, vinegar, and apple
butter. John loved to watch the spring blossoms slowly
turn into the glowing fruit of autumn.

Watching the apples grow inspired in John a love of all of nature. He often escaped from his boisterous household to the tranquil woods. The animals sensed his gentleness and trusted him.

As soon as John was old enough to leave home, he set out to explore the vast wilderness to the west. When he reached the Allegheny Mountains, he cleared a plot of land and planted a small orchard with the pouch of apple seeds he had carried with him.

John walked hundreds of miles through the Pennsylvania forest, living like the Indians he befriended on the trail. As he traveled, he cleared the land for many more orchards. He was sure the pioneer families would be arriving before long, and he looked forward to supplying them with apple trees.

When a storm struck, he found shelter in a hollow log or built a lean-to. On clear nights he stretched out under the stars.

Over the next few years, John continued to visit and care for his new orchards. The winters slowed him down, but he survived happily on a diet of butternuts.

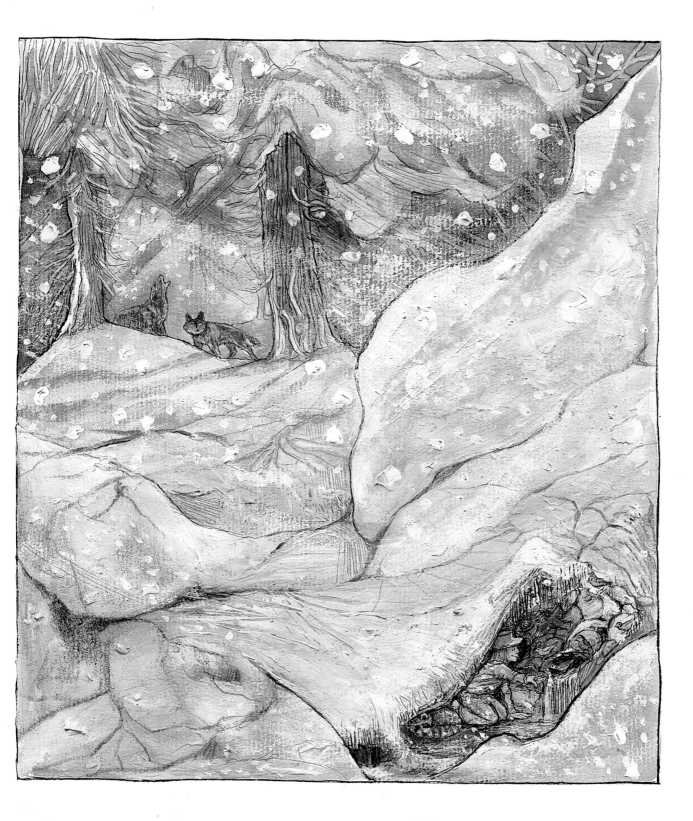

One spring he met a band of men who boasted that they could lick their weight in wildcats. They were amazed to hear that John wouldn't hurt an animal and had no use for a gun.

They challenged John to compete at wrestling, the favorite frontier sport. He suggested a more practical contest—a tree-chopping match. The woodsmen eagerly agreed.

When the sawdust settled, there was no question about who had come out on top.

John was pleased that the land for his largest orchard had been so quickly cleared. He thanked the exhausted woodsmen for their help and began planting.

During the next few years, John continued to move westward. Whenever he ran out of apple seeds, he hiked to the eastern cider presses to replenish his supply. Before long, John's plantings were spread across the state of Ohio.

Meanwhile, pioneer families were arriving in search of homesites and farmland. John had located his orchards on the routes he thought they'd be traveling. As he had hoped, the settlers were eager to buy his young trees.

John went out of his way to lend a helping hand to his new neighbors. Often he would give his trees away. People affectionately called him Johnny Appleseed, and he began using that name.

He particularly enjoyed entertaining children with tales
of his wilderness adventures and stories from the Bible.

In 1812 the British incited the Indians to join them in another war against the Americans. The settlers feared that Ohio would be invaded from Lake Erie.

It grieved Johnny that his friends were fighting each
other. But when he saw the smoke of burning cabins, he
ran through the night, shouting a warning at every door.

After the war, people urged Johnny to build a house
and settle down. He replied that he lived like a king in his
wilderness home, and he returned to the forest he loved.

During his long absences, folks enjoyed sharing their recollections of Johnny. They retold his stories and sometimes they even exaggerated them a bit.

Some recalled Johnny sleeping in a treetop hammock
and chatting with the birds.

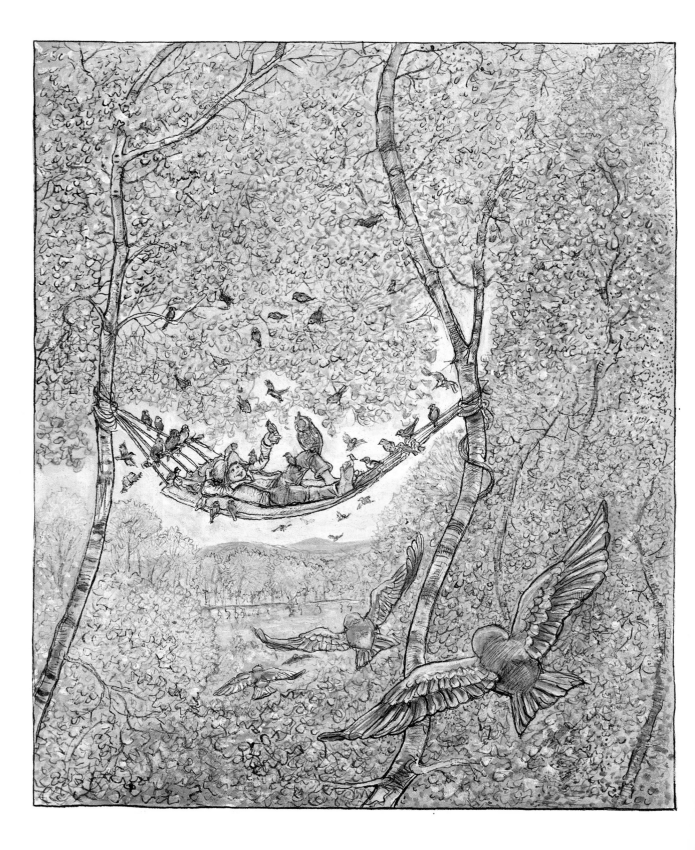

Others remembered that a rattlesnake had attacked his foot. Fortunately, Johnny's feet were as tough as elephant's hide, so the fangs didn't penetrate.

It was said that Johnny had once tended a wounded
wolf and then kept him for a pet.

An old hunter swore he'd seen Johnny frolicking with a bear family.

The storytellers outdid each other with tall tales about his feats of survival in the untamed wilderness.

As the years passed, Ohio became too crowded for Johnny. He moved to the wilds of Indiana, where he continued to clear land for his orchards.

When the settlers began arriving, Johnny recognized some of the children who had listened to his stories. Now they had children of their own.

It made Johnny's old heart glad when they welcomed
him as a beloved friend and asked to hear his tales again.

When Johnny passed seventy, it became difficult for him to keep up with his work. Then, in March of 1845, while trudging through a snowstorm near Fort Wayne, Indiana, he became ill for the first time in his life.

Johnny asked for shelter in a settler's cabin, and a few days later he died there.

Curiously, Johnny's stories continued to move westward without him. Folks maintained that they'd seen him in Illinois or that he'd greeted them in Missouri, Arkansas, or Texas. Others were certain that he'd planted trees on the slopes of the Rocky Mountains or in California's distant valleys.

Even today people still claim they've seen Johnny Appleseed.

AUTHOR'S NOTE

The legends that grew around John Chapman, or Johnny Appleseed, began during his lifetime in the last quarter of the eighteenth and first half of the nineteenth centuries. Since then an enormous amount has been written about him, and I explored much of that literature before beginning my picture-book version of his life and adventures.

I was surprised to learn from R. I. Curtis, a West Virginia historian writing in 1859, that John Chapman had a Bunyanesque talent that allowed him to "chop as much wood and girdle as many trees in one day as most men could in two." In recalling his childhood memories of John Chapman, Curtis wrote: "He was very fond of children and would talk to me a great deal, telling me of the hardships he had endured, of his adventures, and hairbreadth escapes by flood and field."

John Chapman's zestful retellings of his adventures inspired others as well. Henry Howe recorded Johnny Appleseed anecdotes that were circulating in Ohio twenty years after his departure for Indiana. In his *Historical Recollections of Ohio* (1846), Howe described him as a man who "went bare-footed, and often traveled miles through the snow in that way. . . . He was careful not to injure any animal and thought hunting morally wrong. He was welcome everywhere among the settlers, and was treated with great kindness . . . by the Indians."

As the years passed and the stories were reinterpreted and retold, a sentimentalization of Johnny Appleseed became discernible. Soon the identity of the initial inspiration became lost in a highly romanticized outpouring of stories, poems, and plays. An ardent contributor to that metamorphosis was Miss Rosella Rice, a nineteenth-century Ohio novelist who spoke of Johnny Appleseed's "memory glowing in our hearts while his deeds live anew every springtime in the fragrance of the apple blossoms he loved so well."

The facts of John Chapman's life emerged again thanks to the research of Dr. Robert Price, who published his findings in the book *Johnny Appleseed: Man and Myth* (1954). He concluded that "when a folktale attains the status of a myth and embodies a cherished ideal of the people, then its true worth no longer lies merely in the dead facts that may have inspired it, but in the new, living, and creating force that it has become in the present."

In my picture book I tried to weave incidents and images from the frontier life of John Chapman with those that continue to be inspired by Johnny Appleseed, the most gentle, generous, and beloved of America's mythic figures.